First Facts™

The Senses

Hearing

by Rebecca Olien

Consultant:
Eric H. Chudler, PhD, Research Associate Professor
Department of Anesthesiology, University of Washington
Seattle, Washington

Capstone press

Mankato, Minnesota

First Facts is published by Capstone Press,
151 Good Counsel Drive, P.O. Box 669, Mankato, Minnesota 56002.
www.capstonepress.com

Library of Congress Cataloging-in-Publication Data
Olien, Rebecca.
    Hearing / by Rebecca Olien.
    p. cm.—(First facts: the senses)
    Summary: "Explains the sense of hearing and how the ears work as sense organs"—Provided
by publisher.
    Includes bibliographical references and index.
    ISBN 0-7368-4301-9 (hardcover)
    1. Hearing—Juvenile literature. I. Title.
QP462.2.O43 2006
612.8'5—dc22   2004027741

Editorial Credits
Wendy Dieker, editor; Juliette Peters, designer; Molly Nei, illustrator;
    Wanda Winch, photo researcher/photo editor

Photo Credits
BananaStock Ltd., 15
Bruce Coleman Inc./Gail M. Shumway, 20; Michael and Patricia Fogden, 19
Capstone Press/Karon Dubke, cover, 1, 5, 8, 14, 21
Corbis/Joe McDonald, 13
Dan Delaney Photography, 9
Dwight R Kuhn, 12
Photo Researchers Inc./James King-Holmes, 16
Rubberball, 6

1 2 3 4 5 6 10 09 08 07 06 05

Table of Contents

The Sense of Hearing

Your five senses help you know what is around you. Body parts are used to gather information. Messages sent to the brain tell you what is seen, heard, felt, tasted, and smelled.

Ears are body parts that sense sound. Using your ears, you can hear your friend's voice on the phone.

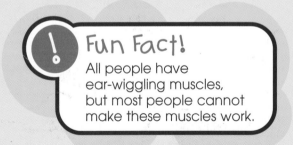

! Fun Fact!
All people have ear-wiggling muscles, but most people cannot make these muscles work.

Sound Waves

When something moves, it moves the air around it too. A guitar string moves, or **vibrates**, when it is plucked. The vibrations move the air around the string. The moving air makes **sound waves**.

Fun Fact!
Sound waves also move through solids and liquids.

The Ears

Ears collect sound waves for us to hear. The outer ear, or **pinna**, is curved to catch sound waves. The pinna's grooves also help collect sound waves.

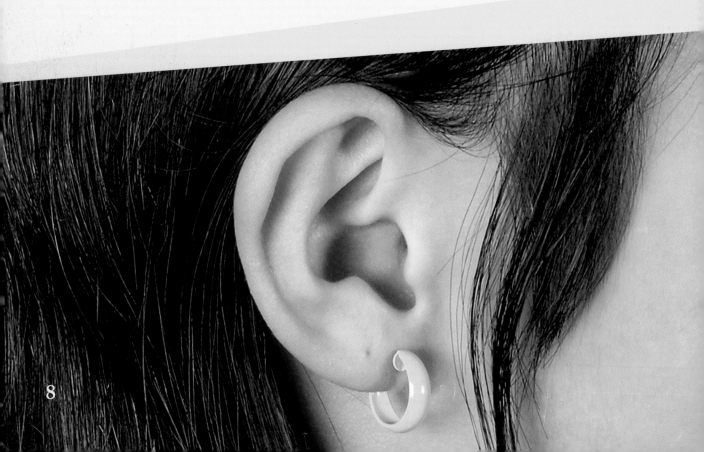

Two ears help you find a sound's location. If a sound comes from the left, your left ear will hear it first. Your brain tells you the sound's location.

Inside the Ear

To hear, sound waves must enter the ear canal. The waves move the eardrum. The wiggling eardrum moves three tiny bones. They are the **hammer**, **anvil**, and **stirrup**.

Next, the stirrup moves fluid in the **cochlea**. The cochlea sends messages along nerves to the brain. Finally, the brain tells you what you hear.

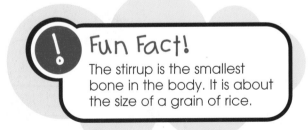

Fun Fact!

The stirrup is the smallest bone in the body. It is about the size of a grain of rice.

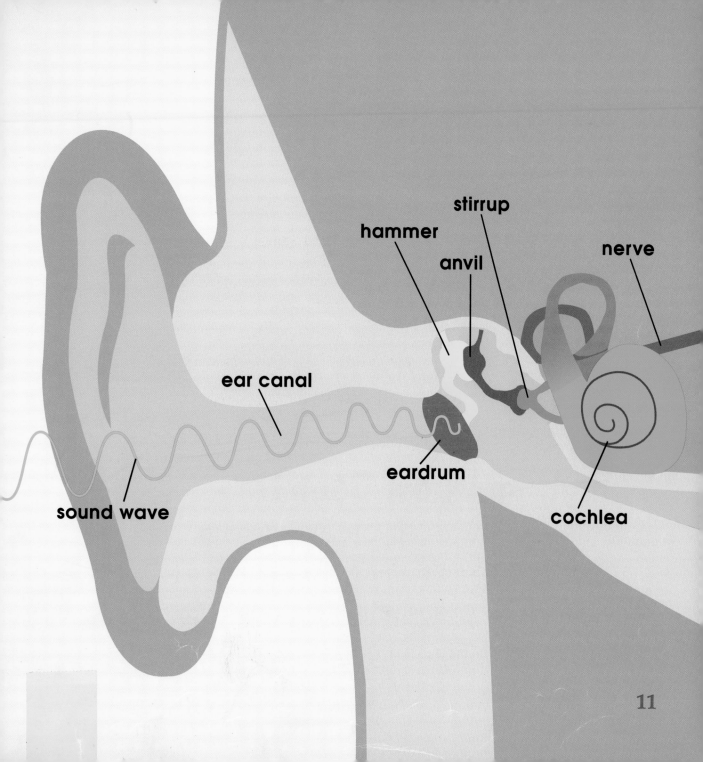

stirrup

hammer

anvil

nerve

ear canal

eardrum

sound wave

cochlea

11

High and Low Sounds

Sound waves vibrate at different speeds. Fast vibrations give sounds a high **pitch**. A mosquito's beating wings buzz with a high pitch.

Slow vibrations give sounds a low
pitch. A toad's croak makes slow
vibrations. Its croak has a low pitch.

Taking Care of the Ears

Loud sounds can damage the ears.
Avoid noisy machines and loud music.
Earplugs can protect your ears from
loud sounds.

Make sure to get your ears checked when you have an earache. Doctors can see if something is wrong.

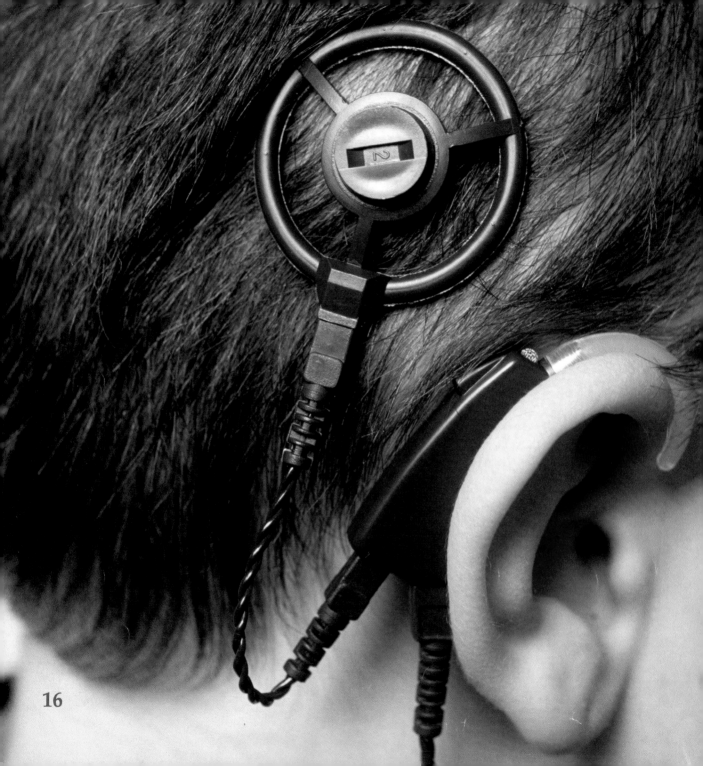

Loss of Hearing

Hearing loss happens when the ear is damaged by loud sounds or sickness. People use hearing aids to hear better.

Other people can't hear at all. Some people can have wires put inside the cochlea. A machine on the head sends sound messages to the cochlea. Then the brain can get sound messages.

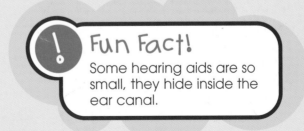

Fun Fact!
Some hearing aids are so small, they hide inside the ear canal.

Bats Use Hearing

Bats have very good hearing. They hear sounds bounce. Bats send out high-pitched sounds. These sounds bounce off objects and go back to the bats' large ears. The bouncing sounds tell bats where the objects are. Bats use bouncing sounds to find insects in the dark to eat.

Fun Fact!

Bat sounds are too high for people to hear. Elephants make sounds that are too low for people to hear.

Amazing but True!

A bird in New Guinea gives scientists clues about how dinosaurs might have communicated. The cassowary's crest helps it make a low booming sound that can travel through the thick rain forest. Scientists think dinosaurs with crests made low sounds too.

Hands On: What Big Ears!

The shape of your outer ear works to gather sound waves. Make bigger outer ears out of paper. See if you can hear better.

What You Need

construction paper
masking tape

What You Do

1. Roll the pieces of paper into cone shapes.
2. Use tape to hold the cones together.
3. Hold the cones next to your ears.
4. Compare how things sound with and without the cones.
5. Experiment by changing the direction that the cones are pointed. Try pointing them up, down, left, and right.
6. Try making other shapes of "big ears." What shapes improve your hearing?

What kinds of animals have large ears? Do you think they hear better than animals with small ears?

Glossary

anvil (AN-vill)—one of the tiny bones in the ear

cochlea (KOH-klee-uh)—part of the inner ear that sends sound messages to the brain

hammer (HAM-ur)—one of the tiny bones in the ear

pinna (PIN-uh)—the outer part of the ear

pitch (PICH)—the highness or lowness of a sound

sound waves (SOUND WAYVS)—movements that travel through air, solids, or liquids that our ears hear as sounds

stirrup (STUR-uhp)—one of the tiny bones in the ear

vibrate (VYE-brate)—to move back and forth quickly

Read More

Cobb, Vicki. *Bangs and Twangs: Science Fun with Sound.* Brookfield, Conn.: Millbrook Press, 2000.

Pringle, Laurence. *Hearing.* Explore Your Senses. New York: Benchmark Books, 2000.

Simon, Seymour. *Eyes and Ears.* New York: HarperCollins, 2003.

Internet Sites

FactHound offers a safe, fun way to find Internet sites related to this book. All of the sites on FactHound have been researched by our staff.

Here's how:

1. Visit *www.facthound.com*
2. Type in this special code **0736843019** for age-appropriate sites. Or enter a search word related to this book for a more general search.
3. Click on the **Fetch It** button.

FactHound will fetch the best sites for you!

Index